Barbies
at communion

& other poems

marcus goodyear

𝓉ß T. S. Poetry Press

T. S. Poetry Press
Ossining, New York
tspoetry.com

Throughout this collection, various poems include references to the following brands: Barbie, a trademark of Mattel; McDonald's, a trademark of McDonald's; Coca-Cola, a trademark of The Coca-Cola Company; M&Ms, a trademark of Mars, Incorporated; F150, a trademark of the Ford Motor Company; Troy-Bilt, a trademark of Troy-Bilt Products; Yamaha Motif, a trademark of Yamaha Corporation of American; Home Depot, a trademark of The Home Depot U.S.A., Inc,; and Styrofoam, a trademark of The Dow Chemical Company.

Cover image by Claire Burge. http://www.claireburge.com/

Scripture taken from the HOLY BIBLE, NEW INTERNATIONAL VERSION. Copyright © 1973, 1978, 1984 International Bible Society. Used by permission of Zondervan Bible Publishers.

ISBN 978-0-9845531-0-5

Library of Congress Cataloging-in-Publication Data:
Goodyear, Marcus
    [Poems.]
    Barbies at Communion and Other Poems/Marcus Goodyear
    ISBN 978-0-9845531-0-5
    Library of Congress Control Number: 2010927331

The author and publisher wish to express their grateful acknowledgment to the following publications and venues in which some of these poems first appeared:

Geez ("Barbies at Communion" and "Easter")
Stonework Journal ("Passion Play" and "Outside Abilene")
32 Poems ("Aubade")
Liturgical Credo ("Waiting for the Shadow to Rise" and "21st Century Kohathites")
Laity Lodge Cody Center ("Garden of Stone and Flesh")
Strange Horizons ("Revolution Day")

Throughout this book are many gift poems.
That is, poems dedicated to a particular person were
almost always given as literal gifts to that person.
This book is dedicated to them, but also to my
parents who taught me to love words.

CONTENTS

FROM THE AUTHOR

I ignore my family to read poetry. That's the joke in my house anyway. Other guys grab a beer, sit on the couch in front of the TV, and respond to every question with grunts: "Uhhnnnhhh Uhhnnnhhh." I grab a beer, sit on the couch to read poetry, and respond with grunts: "Uhhnnnhhh Uhhnnnhhh."

I'm not trying to talk bad about sports fans and beer aficionados. The best of them get up from the couch after the game and head out to the backyard with a ball and mit and a kid at their heels. They turn the solitary game into a social one again.

That's my hope for poetry. I read on the couch, but then I share what I read with my friends and family, just like the sports fan. And like the sports fan, I often make it a game. We create limericks on long drives. We recite Shel Silverstein. My kids see me taking poetry notes during church. They hear me reciting a new poem to test it out on my wife or my parents or whoever happens to be in the room.

Poetry isn't harder than anything else. It isn't scarier. It doesn't need to make anyone feel unintelligent. Poetry is a game of words, stories and images. Of course, there are rules, just like there are rules in baseball. Rules are part of what make a game fun. Of course, there is work involved. If we never practice, we can't expect to show up on game day and play well.

Like any great game, poetry is a kind of deep play that turns us into children again. Poetry is a game of reflection and prayer. Poetry forces us to slow down. It is counter-cultural for our society too. Think about it...

- no one makes much money writing poetry
- there is no *New York Times* Bestsellers List for Poetry— too bad really
- poetry is easy to steal
- poetry is almost meant to be stolen

Poets want people to memorize and internalize their poems. And what could be more like theft than for a poet's words to be inside someone's head, memorized, ready to be recalled at any moment? (Don't worry about stealing my poems. They are all available under a creative commons license.)

To sum up: Poetry is fun. Poetry is sexy. Poetry is cool. Poetry is prayer. Poetry is emotion, but also logic. It is words, but also numbers. It is play, but also work.

And poetry is all around us if we remember to look for it. Poetry is waiting for us just around the corner, in a book on the coffee table, in a phrase from the pulpit, in the wag of a dog's tail, in Barbie dolls and quantum physics and vacations and rituals and work and play. Wherever we go, poetry is playing hide-and-seek with us. Whenever we sit still enough and quiet enough, we can hear poetry shuffling in its hiding place, trying not to make too much noise. But then we throw open the closet door and grab it and make it promise to find us when we try to hide, to always keep the game going.

— Marcus Goodyear 2010

Barbies at Communion

During communion meditation, young men pass
shiny brass plates with saltless crackers
and shots of grape juice and the speaker
compares communion to German McDonald's:
an oasis of comfort in a foreign land?
"We share this meal.
Amen? We share
this meal. We share."
While I smile at his cadence,
my daughter undresses
Ariel Barbie, Tinker Bell Barbie,
and 12-inch generic Sleeping Beauty.
I don't know why Ariel's butt crack
makes me nervous, shining up at me
as I break a corner of cracker, Christ's
flesh passing over naked dolls,
breasts without nipples
like an Eve before shame.

Scribbling

"We have to fly to Georgia
because it's far away."
My daughter spreads wide
her arms and fingers.
"And we'll fly over the slide park
and the children are gonna say,
'Ah, get away!
'Look at that!
'It's an airplane!'
And they'll hide in the dragon cave—
except there aren't real dragons—
just dragon bones
that we use as wood to make fire."
When I turn her dictation into this poem
she watches me write and asks
"Where's the slide park?
Where's the children?"
So I underline the words and she grumbles
at their refusal to be more
than scribbles on a page.
"Where's Georgia?" she asks,
expecting peach glory
and Co-Cola gentility
to rise from the page.

Passion Play

From a step stool my girl drops tabs in 6 cups,
red, yellow, green, orange, blue, and pink.
She tells the Easter story while we wait
for shells to stain. "This is Jesus,"
my girl begins. She's got a red M&M doll,
a McDonald's Happy Meal prize. "Here's the cross,"
she says and displays her popsicle stick
creation from the Baptist egg hunt.
The M&M doll has a clip—so trendy kids
can hang him from their backpack zipper,
I guess. No marketing exec for junk or fast food
foresaw the candy man of sorrows crucified
on my kitchen table, cups of vinegar hissing
disdain around him. In her gospel
Big Bird stands in for both Marys and visits
the crook of my arm. "Here, Daddy, be the tomb."
Elmo rises a creepy soft angel squeezed, tickled
and giggling against my white washed shoulder
"He is not here! He is risen!"
But our Jesus has not. The storyteller forgot
the hanging candy doll—or worse, I fear—
prefers to see him hang there
an acceptable suggestion of sacrifice
reminding us both to dip our hands
in the bunny bowl for Easter M&Ms,
lilies stamped where Ms should be.
Colored shells bleed on our palms
and the candy Christ speaks,
"This is my body. Take and eat."

Paradise High

God slouches at the front of the universe
leaning against his desk, taking roll
with a red pen in his spiral book of life.
He teaches every subject himself,
every grade, every student. He leads
every parent conference appearing
as principal, department head, counselor,
and teacher. At night he walks the halls
alone with a broom and a trash can.
He's not too grand to pick up
the wad of gum some kid mashed
onto a door frame. He's not above
using divine elbow grease to scrub
away bathroom graffiti. Sometimes
he finds drawings of himself
cross-eyed with a caption,
"What a dork!" the picture of a fool.
But every morning he's back
in the cafeteria, handing out
his own body for breakfast
with a pint of 2% milk—
or chocolate if you like.
He wears a Padres ball cap
to keep God hairs out of the food.
He runs the register, too,
though he never makes us pay.
"I'll get this one," he says—
and every time we wonder why
there's a register at all? Why receipts?

When the bells ring, students rush to class
past God the hall monitor into the room
of Mr. God, the teacher. He greets us
by name wherever we are.
But only in his room do we find
a seat while he watches. God's voice
crackles and pops over the PA
during announcements while God
lines up the hooligans in the hall
to assign tardy detentions.
I hold my breath when God walks
the aisles in his classroom collecting
our English themes like prayers.
Dear God, I pray I pass.

Welcoming Summer

Two love bugs mate on my leg
until I draw them off with this
#2 pencil. The pair crawl past
my thumb as I write, then up
to the pink eraser which must taste
funny to tongue buds on their feet.
They fly away, black-legged snow-
flakes. We think of Christmas specials
where painted children catch snow
on tongues to welcome winter.
"Open wide, kids," I say. "There's
never snow in South Texas."
My son plays along and we run
up and down the blacktop lot—
heat rising in waves around us—
we must look a pair of Baptist Johns,
prophesying protein in the desert.
A voice of two calling between
parked cars: "Prepare the way
for summer bugs. Make straight
your tongues for them." Push that
play too far and bugs become God.
All mankind finds salvation in bugs.
And why not? God can raise up
children from rocks and bugs—
even cars with bug-splattered bumpers.

Coaching My First Soccer Game

for Lyle

I forgot the halftime oranges
so my dad left while I gathered
twelve balls—an apostolate of soccer
needing inflation, mechanical inspiration
by needle and compressed rumble
for my team of five.
More balls than feet makes boys
grin when I up-end the bag
and send them rolling. "Attack
those balls," I yell. "Shoot them in."
Between practice and game, Coach Kirk
tells his Mustangs and my Peanuts,
"Have fun!" They did. Three on three.
Four five-minute quarters. Six kids.
One ball. Dark blue shirts versus light
blue. "Go blue!" Parents yelled.
Out of bounds? Stop. Throw it in.
Ian wants to corner kick. Okay.
Rules are less important than play.

The Price of Renewal

for Josef Luptak

The cold hearth may hold fire when the front comes
where the cellist plays. His arms carve the sound,
not for us, not for himself, but just because
the silence must sometimes be filled
with something besides words and squeaking
animals. We hear them by the door, surprised
each time the pinched strings sing
impossibly high. They could be bats or mice,
vermin that incarnate what Bach first said
years ago and again today with a time machine
made from maple and sheep gut and a life
time of learning the skill to speak
and sing and play for the dead.

It Is Never Enough

for Norm and Helena

I am thinking about waves coming into rocky shores,
crashing their way across crooked cliffs like a strange
continuous run of blue and white dominoes.

The Poetry of Money

for Charlie Peacock

There is no paper note in my wallet
(we've abstracted the green abstraction)
just cold plastic and magnet memory
like a black stripe above the box
where I didn't sign my name.
The stripe is a number
for lasers connected to computers
blinking zeroes and ones, more numbers
that talk to the institutions of numbers.
In God the cashier trusts my stripe,
hands me a plastic sack with the milk
for my kids in the morning.
It will collect on my son's chin
and I will dab it with a paper napkin
and he will say, "Don't, Daddy, don't."

The Poetry of Money 2

for Rachel Marks

The tail of the peacock male
shimmers with metallic coins,
the eyes of money winking
beauty's price. What is a poem
worth? Just this feathery spread
melting change into cool rain.

Resort

When the Baker Hotel died,
no one ordered an autopsy
or called the local mortician.
They just left the carcass
at the crossroads where it fell,
bulging brickwalls, gouged eyes,
empty sockets jagg'd with glass.
On coffee break, the local doc
doesn't wonder if he could
save her. Guilt dies without memory
so don't bother picking the bones.
The marrow sold cheap to antique
stores and left rooms mostly hollow.
Shout your name in the stairwell,
the space will keep your voice
until midnight, bubbling in sulfur baths.
whispering at windows not yet broken,
at doors stuck in jams:
Remember me. Remember me.

Ode on Hope

One day, there will be a green river
and a white cliff and the freedom
to walk outside and talk with God
in a place where doors have no locks
and so don't feel much like doors at all.

Hill Country Achilles

Your pulse beats blood against this pillow
each night, the sound in your ears
like footfalls through fresh snow tracking
back to a time in Texas when it fell
just frozen enough for you to step out
and catalog the memory of weather.
Cold can be beautiful when it falls evenly,
but most winters uneven chills cool porches
not doors, freeze begonias not grass.
Mornings frost fences and shingles,
while warm afternoons catch you all
flushing until you unzip thick coats
and wonder if memory serves up lies
like pie. Meringue could cover your town
beneath peaks that brown in the oven.
If you slice out wedges for guests,
they'll ask for the recipe. Just smile.
Take their plate, all crumbs and sugar
splotches too shallow for forks.
The truth is you won't remember how
you made that fluffy white. It couldn't be
snow. Perhaps the puffed petals of winter
flowers, roses grown to tall green stems
in glass houses that hope for summer
nights when cicadas pray, "Sleep tight."

Zombie Gratitude

for Merrie Destefano

A cup of cold water puts off headaches
and heartaches and all kinds of aches,
dried-out and alone in this place
where some attack us with laughter
until we shuffle away, moaning for brains
like our own to devour. Their spongy meat
tastes sweet to dry tongues, loosens
the lies about what we deserve.

A Beautiful Girl Like You

Polar bear barometers wander
slushy ice shelves, paws sinking,
their world melting. Liquid
water always kills the green-
skinned witch, hissing, shrieking,
What a world. What a world.
Look what beauty can do.
Hear the soldier's silence.
All are free, no longer
servants but friends of beauty,
tigers and bears. Click your ruby
shoes. The mercury is rising.

Aubade

We are sixteen again,
your lips on my neck, your breath
a promise like warm steel.

Impatience

Wedding bed scraped and polished
into a coffee table against its purpose
created in some past eastern dynasty.
A couple came together here
and found life in the pleasures
of mouth on mouth, fingers, shoulders.
These hand-carved curves now
hold laptops and notes and bronze
statues of shepherd boys.
Too many men gather round
on couches to talk shop and God.
Mugs thunk against wood where
the woman lay. Her sweat soaked
in here. Work has life and pleasure
but impatience wants to sweep
everything off and make room
for something more base, a truth
that burns and stains and shudders.

Rudder and Seam

Sometimes when the tea's too hot,
I unwrap the string from the handle
of the mug, where I've rigged
the square paper tag like a flag
hoisting the bag to halfmast,
this caffeine free bliss, not one whit
bitter, not one lick needing sugar,
until I trace my tongue along seam
where mesh hides leaves and spice.
I am Poseidon beneath this lady ship,
no rudder can steer her clear from me.

Revolution Day

for Amy Goodyear

Under French and Swiss, it loops
straddling resistance and neutrality
in tunnels that are many stories
tall. They'll accelerate particles.
Who knows what that means—
except their white coats and access keys.
The Higgs particle could be in reach.
OK. Signatures of supersymmetry, too.
Right. I say, accelerate this family.
Send mom round the rings.
Counter-rotate dad and kids
all of them riding seven trillion
electron volt beams like some carnie
just set it up in a mall parking lot:
"6 tickets a ride, or get a wristband."
Start the flight that ends with smash.
We'll all super-collide to find immensity,
energy, strange answers to strangers'
questions. Asymmetry's embedded here
in the universe—even families—even moms.
Somebody chose what stays and what goes.
Dark matter, gone. Life, the universe,
everything has 23 per cent dross, so mom
lick your finger, smudge the cheek of all
existence and say, Smile for the camera.

Captain Depth Perception

I see you like space
between my car and the raised
bumper of an F150 sitting
wider than yellow parking lines.
I know when to brake and back
up, when to cut the wheel
so I turn just far enough
into your space, filling it
with so much of myself that
almost I fill it all, almost
I feel the crunch of fender and truck.
My power saves
paint jobs at a price.
Every hero has her heal.
Mine's the depth I can't stop
sensing, a constant knowledge
of our world packed tight,
nearing collision, and the fear
of someone cutting too sharp,
closing the space completely.
At night I know twin lights
of speeding cars enough
to pull out and see we're safe
in our sufficient depth of space.

Catch

I've read of people who measure light
as it refracts through holes and sprays
patterns on a screen. What does it mean,
this probability wave, numbers they sketch
into a metaphor so my mind can grasp.
If you look too close, you find certainty
and stamp the wave flat, condense
the mystery of choice into chosen.
What might be withers into what is.
Each moment can disappoint, these sweaty
hands, this stuffy room, bland food,
a touch, a kiss. Decisions risk
everything on black. Spin the wheel,
the steel ball hops and turns and we
watch the wave, catch our breath.
Hope is a ripe apple. Desire, fresh.

Parable of the Sower

Judgment comes like weeds
in a lawn where the mower
sets his machine so low
it scalps the grass
and makes room for ugly
broad leaf and dollar weeds
and worse—prickles and stickers
that turn the outside wild
again, a place we can't walk
bare foot. Slip-on sandals
aren't even enough unless
our feet calluses are
so thick we can't feel
the spines and poisons against
the sides of our soles.
But then we plow through fields
like grounded bees spreading seed,
sowing forms of life we'd never choose,
the fallen world redeemed by our shoes.

Outside Abilene

The land less flat than I
guessed, it's still hairy gray
with curly pubic oak
at the 33-miles-to-go sign
where that church boy fell asleep
and killed a family of four
on their way camping.

Still alive, the land has its labors
pushing until the grain crowns
golden ripe for the combine,
elevated or spewed onto trains
running parallel to barbed wire
stretching between corrugated iron
posts that keep us company.

A sign in the dry lake:
Please Jesus send rain.
But Jesus hitched a ride
in the back of our truck
where the wind blows his dark hair
so wild no one sees him smile
except the dry prickly pear.

Mowing Dead Grass after Church on Sunday

Stubborn life knows no rest.
Our desert lawn grows tall enough
to tickle my fat dog's chest
in just one week. I don't water
and still it grows, not green, not
lush, not Whitman's fresh cut
hair of graves, but burrs and tentacle
grass like dead spiders, brittle
brown in the heat. No poet's passed
here under my army surplus boot-
soled feet, but the dead demand
attention from suburban morticians
trimming the nails of corpse plots
with coughing, greasy Troy-bilts
hacking, at the highest setting,
their zombie lawns, flinging mulched
stickers into shins. Here's the truth,
I'll admit my sin. I love this Sabbath
work, my mower's loud drone
swallows the noisy world whole.

The Garden in Drought

Annuals explode orange and yellow
petals, springing up out of mass-
packaged manure compost and mulch,
watered, loved, weeded, and eaten
one night by scrawny white-tailed
yard rats. So we content ourselves
with less flashy flora. Plant bitter
herbs, pungent rosemary, sweet
basil. Small doses grow slow, but
the earth's best beauty endures
even when subtle tastes are lost
on calloused tongues. Stark life
is life unadorned, and passion
doesn't shout amen or raise hands.
We're not lukewarm. We're salt. Our faith
is breath and heartbeat. Our cups
run over, but they're still just cups.

Drought on the Open Road

Once the herd was so thirsty
they ate the burn right off
the interstate shoulder, two bites
from asphalt and cars flying
75 miles to nowhere.
Heat paralyzed cows
never look up.

Garden of Stone and Flesh

Frankie and Fran divorced and left a villa
in a cul de sac. Fran's weekend work bought the wrought
iron fence, each bar topped by a bulbous spike.
Frankie's commission checks purchased a garden
of gray concrete statues, a Parthenon mass-
produced for discount home improvement stores.
Lions flanking the driveway sphynxed Aunt Jane
walking by, her dog pulling at the leash to escape
the strangle of concrete riddles. Benches
like empty thrones sat in the yard waiting
for some gardening god to rest, the cold stone
a shock to any divine backside. Concrete
deer and elephants, frogs and gnomes, and a mermaid
and children with stone stares missing pupils,
lacking focus. Static gods, immutable, hard.
Like Frankie and Fran who turned to stone, pupils empty,
cold in a garden where no children played, no couple loved
to imagine new figures filling each patch
of empty grass so the house sold in settlement.
The new owners' children play Father Time
with hammers, knocking off noses and arms and heads
until dad wraps a rusty chain around each
statue's neck and drags them one by one
behind his riding mower out to the curb
next to the trash cans and recycle bins and mail.
A week later his kids watch bulk pickup
park and scoop the pile with hydraulic jaws
"Like Mike Mulligan's steam shovel," says their dad.

"Or Aslan," says his oldest. It must be an evil Aslan
who holds his breath and eats Narnia's dead.
The youngest son's wide brown eyes watch each gray
body fall in the truck with a crash of dust.
And dad wonders what life could hide in stone.

Ars Moriendi

The confused worm spun a web
in darkness under the bathroom
sink—a strange place for transformation
next to cleaning supplies and dop
kits for business trips. Thank God
we opened the cabinet door
for a new tube of toothpaste
and one morning freed a moth.

Epiphany

We put our Jesuses in the attic
after Christmas, buried in boxes
between plastic wreaths and cheap lights.
I rarely think about the idle figures
when I fetch luggage for business trips.
Near the boxes, the space is a maze
of pipes wrapped in thin foam, too thin
for January freezes when water reminds us
who is in charge. So here I am,
my breath like a pillar of cloud.
When the pipes crack, the water sprays.
There is no controlling this flood
and the damage it causes, soaking
through our Christmas, baptizing Santas,
Rudolphs, wreaths, and every single Jesus.

Prayer Partners

I need prayer, absolution, all that, but
I also need a bathroom. So I pee
in the stall next to an artist
whose oils I saw last night.
"Dude, I loved your art," I say.
He doesn't respond but we hear
each other's water. "Especially,"
I say, "the one with the black tree
on the right." He grunts acknowledgment
and I'm still peeing damn coffee.
"And the one with the red skulls.
My son would love that one."
I wash my hands first, then grab
too many paper towels. "Thanks," he says.

Parable of the Healer

Years ago when medicine was urine
and moss and mud packs with ground worms,
people died at twenty-seven, and one
third of all people died of the plague
every thirty years. Healing was a mystery,
God's business, entrusted to God because
clearly the urine cakes did not work.
And thirty years later when lymph
nodes swelled black again with pestilence,
they must have wondered if God wasn't
a little too much like a urine cake.

Sunday Morning at the Donut Palace

for Bill Edwards

The old men believe in nothing
but humanity and an empire
of experience. They love the teens
selling donuts in summer, and coffee,
frying pastries earlier than English
ever was, finding cheap freedom
in time at the register
turning to cash. Honest to God,
they learn the truth of green linen
from patriarchs long dead, framed and stained
by sweaty hands from hundreds who
handed them out, passed them over,
sounded the old bell, Ka-Ching! Enjoy
your coffee, sir. Have a nice day.
What's not to love? Kids work hard
and make bread too sweet to be holy
sacraments or exodus memories.
God floods the world, and he doesn't
like sprinkles or chocolate or maple,
even plain glaze is too glazed to be plain.
On the floor you can eat bland manna,
back where the manager forgot to sweep,
miracle crumbs and dust by our feet.
The old men laugh and don't believe it,
not for one second. Life is good,
but life ends and nothing waits
in the dirt but more earth.

A Boy Becomes Like God

My dog ran out
to chase a motorcycle
speeding through
the neighborhood.
Never expected
to catch it
with her puppy head
and a short yelp
that left her
breathing slow
looking scared.
On the back porch
we wrapped her
in black plastic
we had bought
for grass clippings,
but I didn't cry
until I carried the bag
to the curb for the dead
animal pickup
and felt her inside
the three-ply trash sack
furry and cold and stiff.
I had touched death before
on my waxy grandma
but death took a puppy
to touch me.

Half of the Hike

A limestone cliff shows the end of the climb
though most never notice the gradual incline
that leads us here. Each step feels more or less
normal, doesn't wind us or try us. We pass
boulders without stopping and mossy logs.
When our tired legs catch on tree roots,
we blame the terrain's loose rocks. On top,
we snap shots. A man checks his watch.

Bird Watching

for Scot McKnight

It must be a kind of faith
projection. I'm agnostic today
but I see devotion in the calm
at the corners of a man's
mouth, eyes masked by matte
black binoculars. Birds are nice,
you understand, but I don't soar
with them even in dreams.
I used to dream of jumping,
catching the wind at my chest,
and arching into flight. Now
only my legs fly behind me
when my dream self
claws at the ground.

2 Guys Making a Bookshelf

for Rick Lane

We buy bulk lumber, browsing tall stacks of wood
all morning looking and sorting, through pine boards,
rejecting ones with knots or gouges, though we mar
what we buy later, tripping on extension cords
plugged into a table saw, a sander, a paint gun,
a shop vac, a drill, tripping on little bits of leftover
wood blocks and shavings and slivers, or the wood
itself assembled into shelves, drying on the floor
like sleeping warriors, and we are monsters creeping
through their drop cloth tent, where they dance and sing
stories of epic bookshelves: the quick one for scrap
booking paper, the first one for California paperbacks,
the planned one to fill the wall like art. But this Christmas
Rick's garage sings of the double-sided bookshelf,
Great Home Depot's son, who rose from lumber
until two men could barely lift him. With molding soldiers
wielding half inch # 6 screws, the great warrior rode
a truck bed into new concrete country, just east of far west.
"Good bookshelves make good neighbors," I say as we walk
the final product, blowing sawdust with puffed cheeks,
noticing imperfections, paint drips, black cracks. Rough edges
our sander missed. Doubt rises like God-cursed Grendel
who hates all joy and oral literature—what these shelves
may hold after another set of brackets to secure the seven
inch wide one-by-eights. "We could fill that crack
with caulk," he says if time and patience weren't short.
But we're done, except cleaning I'd hoped to help with.

He knows his tool spots, though, and he loves projects.
I bag up paint plastic, splattered with Doubt's white blood—
my bookshelf ripped Doubt's arm off at the shoulder joint,
twisting Doubt's wrist, until sinews stretched to tearing
and the white burst, spraying our shelves in victory,
honor and glory recorded in verses they'll sing until
Doubt's mother raises the garage door seeking revenge.

Community Theater

for Jeff and Heather Cunningham

I'm no magi, and I'm no longer
at ease here in the old dispensation,
mediocre buildings with parking
lots filled each Sunday. Smiles
shake hands, butts fill pews, mouths
shape air into words and air and
words. What's been dispensed
except these silk ties, brass
collection plates, stained glass
overlooking trapsets, amplifiers
and the Yamaha Motif keyboard
on its hydraulic stand. Can we go?
I'm just tired. It's almost noon
and the community theater needs
me backstage for the matinee.

The Problem with Grace

for Steven Purcell

Don't apologize. Wipe away
your planks and beams.
Look closer, past the dust.
Words become a box
canyon and someone took
the rope. Your only prayer
is a hermeneutic of charity
notched into the rock, common
grace in shadows and toe holds.
But also something prowling
just beyond the lip of this
short cliff. Its teeth are a broken
jail that cannot contain
animal rage and hunger.
Place your left foot here.

Evangelism 101

Who needs nets when we can
catch our fish in yellow boxes
stamped with names like inulin
and L-Carnitine? Yet we still fish
for men the old way, cast out
worms and hooks. Our bait is slimy.
Our methods leave scars. "Go away
from us, Lord. We have sinned."
Our words are a bluff for God
to show his hand, throw the game
in our favor, and lose the pot.
Send us home with winnings enough
to celebrate, take our wives out
for scampi or oysters on the half shell,
offering their flesh to our teeth.

Christ Is Risen, But

for John Wurster

I'm certain that worms dig tunnels,
crawl in, crawl out of the doubter's mouth.
Without questions, we never find answers.
Without decay, life is not renewed.
Faith doesn't turn tadpoles into frogs,
and worms spin cocoons from doubt, not hope,
stitching themselves into darkness, disbelieving
(for joy) their uncertain metamorphosis
that wraps them up in sticky wings. Wonder
disturbs the best sales pitch, confident
of promised flight in open Sopwith Camels.
The barnstormer's stick shifts between
our legs, guided by the unseen mover
whose feet turn rudders until we lose
our stomachs, our whoop lost in
the rushing wind. Where the mystery is
too great, give us flesh.

Prayer for the Pompadour Looking up from My Plate

God, I feel bad.
He died for me
and I could only
eat half of him.

Listen

for Carroll

I'm conducting faeries
with a femur I found
in the bamboo forest
between the golf course
and the world.

The Collectors

for Charles and Rebecca Trois

"What do you collect?" she asks
because everyone collects something—
Barbies, children, cars, beer, wine,
movies, diamonds, dogs, dresses, bits
of flat screen plasma—and boots
like turrets above the TV, the skulls
were Ozzie's, and this picture of a Native
American princess I should know,
the dress she wore in sepia tones hangs
full color in a glass cabinet, a book in plastic
jacket tells her story next to the model train
on the pool table. This place is a home
with snarling dead monkey-head lamps,
and Saint Michael guards the door—
his sword shines white miracles—
Frankish armor from an age
when even the dust shined, empty
barrels, breast-bared figureheads from
a ship front, the Maharaja's emerald,
an amber skull believe it or not.
And his pop gun museum with the oldest
and rarest, not the same mind you,
and my favorite, the spy kid kit
complete with pistol, badge, and silencer.
Picasso and guns, steam engines and treaty
photos of a trusting tribe posing

before another Manifest Destiny swindle.
In the hall, each medal is another
broken treaty. We collect lies
and words and Hautzi Nazi pin cushions
"He who sticks gets stuck in the end"
or in a coffin. The miniature Hitler lies
in state, slide the lid back with a finger,
like this see? Watch out for his quarter-
inch erection, spring loaded for a laugh.
Poems bring order, so I collect flashes
of sense and will, turn whimsy just so,
find morals in monkey-head lamps:
my body is a brick. Take and create.

Easter

I found Jesus in the shower
behind the church pulpit
in the green room built for brides.
I don't know why he was there
his Styrofoam self crucified, crooked
against tiles, one arm poking past
the creased anti-mildew curtain.
He must have been part of a catalog
package deal—between Advent candles
and bulk host—buy the cross,
get the Jesus. The cross
someone painted faux wood
and mounted stage left,
empty "because Jesus rose."
The Styrofoam Jesus, no one painted.
His grimace a ghostly bleached white
waits in that back room for someone
like me to notice while standing to pee
Jesus Christ! in the shower.

Regional Grace

Commuters jump Pacific-sized puddles
on thin wings and jet props cocking
one arm against the cabin's steel curve.
Sail boats below carve white scars
in the blue, working with the wind we fight.
The boy in front of me can't walk on water
yet. He grabs the arm rest, flashes a tooth-
gritted grimace and feels each fall.

21st Century Kohathites

*After Aaron and his sons have finished covering the holy furnishings
and all the holy articles, and when the camp is ready to move, the
Kohathites are to come to do the carrying. But they must not touch the
holy things or they will die. The Kohathites are to carry those things
that are in the Tent of Meeting. (Numbers 4:15)*

We carry a broken truth,
dissembled logic, wrapped in skins,
seals and goats sacrificed
served with figs, so their bodies
protect some piece of word.
I'm not carrying some Sunday
School Jesus, and I'm not afraid
to untie leather straps and peek.
My unholy hands unfold the wiry pelt.
My eyes are burned with lust—
images of every cheap and hasty coupling.
My mouth breathes the sour stench of stale
coffee, coating my teeth with yellow.
My songs of praise under my nose stink.
Fire from heaven never falls in truth
on men who seek the truth in fear—
because the word is a scaly confession
spreading leathery wings and breathing
fresh air into this chest like an oven
heating inspiration to greasy flames.

Sacrifice

Once upon a teenage midnight,
outside martial grade school walls,
a Christian girl took him down
inside the moat long dry
so that swing sets grew
in narrow playing fields
for toddler soccer and tag.
Beyond the lamps on a fort
he sat and she sat
on his lap and let her
cotton dress ride up.
Clouds covered stars for hours.
Parking lot puddles are weightless
liquid, unseen ripples traveling
circles in lapping rhythms.
Lips will melt wet stone.

Watching the Shadow Rise

Adam and Eve were quite complicit.
She offered the fruit.
He ate it.
And it was good
at first. Dusk behind them,
they sat in the garden
and watched the shadow rise
up the eastern ridge
turning their backs to bright
colors, savoring blues, purples, blacks
where stars shine first
with messages of light across years
of light before e equaled anything
except this raw shared sweetness
and the potential of double-crusted
pie, fritters, sauce, a red jewel
in the mouth of a roasting pig.
God provides the sacrifice. We
always eat it.

Yoked Together

At night I hike
on rocks, my thoughts
collecting as I walk,
like sticker burrs on socks,
or daddy long leg
crowds clinging to box
canyon walls. If I brush
those sleeping spiders,
they dance and spread,
a patch of hair come to life.
I have been here before.
Held this rope to climb.
Fit my toes in notches,
watched another's ascent,
wished for a fall
the way I sometimes want
to twist the wheel
when I drive, crash
through bushes and barbed
wire fences to freedom flights.

Eve's Second Garden

Filled with succulents and spines
that scratch her legs and break
off inside, so Adam has to pinch
her skin, then suck and bite
the sliver, his teeth the only tweezers
yet invented. Nothing requires much
water. Five months drought each winter
turns prickly pears brilliant purple
before they die. Yucca shade hides
the snakes, so she rustles the grass
with a sotol stalk. Frightened, they rattle.
She freezes and listens to them promise,
"Our kisses turn you brilliant purple."

Practice Is an Art

for David Tolley

The pianist plays alone everytime—
learning not to let the world decide
when he creates and when he rests.
Studios, concert halls, practice rooms
hallowed, not hollow, never empty.
The walls, the chairs, the carpet tremble
with potential, their voices hushed
waiting for the performer's approach.
He clacks the cover from its keyboard,
coughs once and begins to say this
I am.
Meaning something more than self,
more than These hands are mine. These legs
pump pedals, sustain notes, build chords.
This room was not empty before.
I have not filled it except with thanks.
Though as for that, no thanks
depends on him or the one listening,
who wandered into the studio looking
to kill time and fighting music instead.
The battle lost, the audience slumps
low in the back row and hears
practice give voice to everything here.

Yet Another Heresy

We all know the truth in our hearts.
Moses in the desert was a weak piss
nobody admires. Running from royal problems,
poor middle-aged shepherd man.
Forget him. I want to burn and burn—
like those star people with comet lives
that streak their names across the sky,
then live in bushes down below
and burn and burn and never slow.

Wrestling with the Father

Freud said there were no jokes.
In the beginning was the joke,
the hidden truth, words too bitter
to be real. Preface life with a half laugh.
Game's on. We're just playing, messing
around with heads and expectations.
I like to wrestle with Pop. He tackles
my waist and throws me. I hook
an elbow around his calves, knock him
to his knees—our breath intense and thick,
our cheeks pressed against cheap berber.
A poke in the side and our grunts turn serious.
Authority's upset—pushed too far.
No names will change, but we are fighting
with God and we are winning
whether we like it or not.

Sabbath

Shed no tears for these empty buildings
around the grass field like a private
forgotten park. They will not feel lonely
next week when a new group arrives
on the wings of petroleum and expectation.
Sometimes emptiness lets us all rest
a bit and take a breath. Throw sticks
for fat dogs who run until their panting
clicks, and they wobble, drunk on fetch,
behind the boy on his way to the river
to dangle his feet in clear water
where no one has come today to swim.

As the Deer

We owe it to each other
to share what white tail already know.
When the pressure changes, they run
together, hooves clacking across asphalt,
then silent on the dewy lawns.

Also from T. S. Poetry Press

Contingency Plans: Poems,
by David K. Wheeler

A great poet confounds me; he uses the same materials I do —
words — but where I've built a fort, he has erected a cathedral.
Wheeler has "revealed the space behind our ribs," and I must
remove my sandals.

— Susan Isaacs, author *Angry Conversations with God*

Infused with the sort of holiness discovered in that quiet place
behind the mighty waterfall, or staring straight up into the
outstretched arms of a Ponderosa pine.

— Karen Spears Zacharias, author of *Will Jesus Buy Me a
Double-Wide?*

God in the Yard: Spiritual Practice for the Rest of Us,
by L.L. Barkat

Mix Richard Foster and Annie Dillard in a blender, and you'll
pour out *God in the Yard...*

— Ginger Kolbaba, editor Christianity Today's *Kyria*

L.L. Barkat's wise words move us more deeply into matters of
consequence.

— David Naugle, author *Reordered Love, Reordered Lives: Learning the
Deep Meaning of Happiness*

Available in e-book and print editions